When You Don't Know Who You Are

by

Alinda Dickinson Wasner

When You Don't Know Who You Are

Poems ©2016 by Alinda Dickinson Wasner
all rights reserved by the author

Cover art based on a drawing by Kristina Kozlitina
neferet122.deviantart.com

Crisis Chronicles #80
ISBN: 978-1-940996-32-5
1st edition, 1st printing

Published 17 March 2016 by
Crisis Chronicles Press
3344 W. 105th Street #4
Cleveland, Ohio 44111
crisischronicles.com
ccpress.blogspot.com
facebook.com/crisischroniclespress

Contents

"Writing...involves a kind of retreat...trying to find our true selves, both then and now."

—Henning Mankell

When You Don't Know Who You Are

You can make things up—
Are you French they ask?
Russian? Jewish?
Why not? Everyone's
Seen you before anyway
Say you have a twin!
At this point you must have been
Separated at birth from octuplets
Even the hygienist at the dentist's
Office
Says there's another patient
Looks just like you
Swears you to secrecy
When she pulls up the chart.
Well, maybe a slight resemblance
You nod, noting the disparity
But that's part of it, I suppose,
Having to please someone else
On the off chance
That someday you could
Find family
Not have to scan the crowds
At Big Ten games
Instead of catching
The play-by-play
Never mind the times
You convinced yourself
That you'd know them
When you saw them
And they you
Only to not even recognize
Your very own son
As he walked straight
Toward you that time
You visited him at boot camp
He in his army fatigues
And you in his favorite blue dress
And though he was
Old enough not to be
Embarrassed to kiss his mom

In public, he was still too young
To admit he'd been wrong
About the military
That he couldn't really
Get his mind around killing.
But you could read his face.
And so you stood there
In the middle of the parade grounds
Hugging and hugging
Until the shriek of whistles
And a bullhorn
And threat of court martial
Forced you off the field—
Both of you
Knowing you'd found
Something
You didn't know
You'd been looking for
All along.

Faith

Though she says she does not
believe most of it, my grandmother
kneels beside me in church each Sunday,
tickling my arm with the lace
on her handkerchief, the one with
nickels knotted into the corner
so I will have something
to put into the offering plate.

I don't know when I first
notice that some of the stained
glass windows are worse
than my nightmares,
or when I first understand
that the story of King Solomon
and the two mothers
isn't quite right.

But Grandmother says not to worry,
that the day they drove
all the way from the farm
to the Courthouse
through a hundred-year flood
to get me, praying they wouldn't
be late, even the angels
must have been nervous.

Still, my adoptive mom
refuses to discuss it,
and even though my grandfather
likes to tell how he
warmed me inside his shirt
all the way back home
because he loved me,
at first sight,
I keep seeing that moon,
swollen, on the horizon
their only source of light.

But whenever the aunts

whisper in the kitchen
or the uncles
whistle the sad tunes
they say they can never
remember the words to—
whenever Father Cyprian
gets to the part about Abraham and Sarah,
I know that my mom
longs for miracles,
believing that if only she
prays hard enough
God will undo
what an Ohio doctor
did to her
when she was a girl
because he was too drunk
to identify her appendix.

And, like her,
I really want to believe
there's a chapter in the Bible
we haven't heard yet,
one which says it would be
perfectly natural
to want to hack Lana Seminski's
tongue in half
for telling me what no one
ever wanted me to know
in the first place—
that somewhere there is a God
who can take two halves of a baby
and put it together so
everything will be perfect
once again.

So Her Phone's Out

And the wires down
Trees uprooted
Box elder leaves sticking to the windshield
Like fool's gold
But damned if
I'm not here now
Pressing the elevator
To the third floor
And ring her buzzer
Thinking fuck it anyway
40 years and she never
Tried to make contact
But screw the probate judge
Who said he'd never
Open the records
Though all his secretaries and
Interns
Can read the details
Pretend not to stare at me
Over the tops of their glasses
As if this were
A case of incest
Or maybe something
More unspeakable
But here we go now
And let's just see
What excuses
She'll try
To think up this time.

Soaring

Storm-gray twist of sheet birds
mama wrestling at the clothesline,
don't let her *excap*e them,
make her know now

neighbor kids am follow
in they singsong
we-know-something-you-don't—
real-mom-ain't-wanting-keep-you

make her saysay they were lying, say
talk about it now this minute, no, not later
later never never,—too late, later
if only you could priest or

just be Catholic! if Jesus could be bastard, too
hold you in his bosom,
Holy Mother lifetime weeping
and Hell iced over just you

skating! Saint of Skating
Saint of Bridges, Tongue to ice words
Frozen heart of water
Cover ears when best friend whisper

Her own dirty secret: born with no vagina, doctors promise
Make her new one when she eighteen—
husband never know the samesame
God of all UnKnowing, God of Saying Nothing

silence turn you crazy, make you pick
the wrong day, sunny,
kneel beneath the clothesline,
praying clouds and fury, wind enough

to slap the sheets out
slap you out of dreaming
make you neck into a knot-knot,
both you soon be soaring.

When You Don't Know Who You Are, Part 2

You can leave the conference early
And drive all the way to Zanesville

In a driving rain
The leaves plastering themselves like fool's gold

To your windshield
Little court jesters

That would like to see you
Swerve off the road into the Muskingum

Sort of a Welcome-to-McConnelsville Waltz

The dial turned to WCZY and Connie Francis
And then Old Blue Eyes

And how ironic, you think
Takes you back to the time Howard Runyon

Wanted you to lift your shirt for him
Saying all the other girls did

But you pushed him off you
Because you didn't want your own kid

To have to be adopted.

When You Don't Know Who You Are, Part 3

You can screw up your courage
And tell the probate judge

That fuck the fact
He's on the bench for life

He's screwed you for the last time
By not opening your records

But his secretary
And his file clerk

Can sit right there in front of you
Flipping through your file

And looking at you
Like they're glad they're not you

Even though they've just
Complimented you on your hair and heels

As if you're now some kind of alien
As if they're ever so very very glad

They didn't have to petition an asshole
For forty years to no avail

And one of them, you can tell
Would probably leave the folder

Right out where you could reach it
Because it's not really sealed

With some grand golden seal
Of wax impressed with the judge's

High school ring
Class of 1933 as he would have you believe

And run out the door and down the steps

Of this monster institution
With its phony scales of justice

And sit in your car and read it
And throw it out the window

When the police try to stop you
Try to write a ticket

For grand theft larceny
Or whatever the hell

They write tickets for
When you steal your own records

Even if there are things in there
You both agree you have a right to know.

You can march right up to the third floor
Knock on her door

And say I tried to call but your phone was out
And I was tired of waiting almost 30 years

To hear from you
So here I am

And she can either slam the door
In your face

Or say howdy-do
I've been expecting you

And ask if any of your children are dark
Or if you can fix her computer

Or if you'd like some pie
And pie is all she eats these days

And says she played the piano
At the Methodist church

17

But they sent her to the home for unwed mothers
Where she had to diaper the hydrocephalics

And if the nuns wanted to punish her
They certainly did a grand job of it

But she never told your father
Who was married to the woman

Who beat him on the head
With her stiletto and left him for dead

And your brother died in infancy
But, no, she never married

At least not for long
It wasn't in the stars

But now you're here
She's not gone to lunch in a coon's age

And would you be so kind
To take her?

Red, it was
That stiletto.

*

She's Here Now

every morning in the bathroom mirror
staring out at me,
complete stranger
though I seem more erect
than she was
the first time I met her
and I ask
who the hell are you?
and what are you doing here?
but I know enough
about DNA
to know what a narcissist is
and why I stand staring
and I know she
deserved it when the 200-pound wrestler
died on top of her
and it took her three hours
to crawl out from under
people don't talk
about these things
in polite company
but my sister
who is convinced
that I got the best end
of the deal,
takes a long drag
and lets the smoke out slowly
from her nostrils
like the Welsh Red
we both heard about
in foster care
while her shoe
dangles from the toes
of her foot
the one that will
have to be amputated
by the time she is sixty
but we're all too familiar
with amputations
and that one doesn't scare us

any more than
all the others.

Double Exposure 1

You are in Columbus in the place where the sky
Intersects the railroad track you suddenly realize this is
Not the only time you have been here something about the way
The town is divided along all these angles and then you remember
The woman who took you down the steps into the tunnel
Beneath the court house and the man in the uniform took your name
Out of the vault and opened the book on top of the glass
So that you could see finally who you were, but the lights
Were making zig-zags across your retina and all you could
See were splashes of silver. Later, when you try to go
Back there the bus driver tells you the court house was
Torn down in 1954 some of the records are still missing.
He is lighting a cigarette but the doors of the bus
No longer open because there are too many trains here.

Double Exposure 2

You are in Toledo and you have just stopped for the light
In the place where the road curves under the overpass and
Suddenly the man in the blue neon shorts appears in the rear view
Mirror and then all the cars start honking because the light
Is green but he is the same man you saw driving the bus
You can tell by the face and the angle of his sunglasses
And you follow the street as far as it goes although it is only a circle.
So you get out of the car and you go in and out of all the buildings but
Things are under construction and by the time you find your way back
The man in the blue shorts is gone but something inside your
Heart hurts because you really need to be certain. Later,
When you go back there, you will cut your hair off. You will
Wear sunglasses so you will not be reminded how blue the sky is
When he's no longer there.

Oh, She Said

Yes, and that was your father
the dark one
whose eyes held until you
had to look away
but something
about the blond one
the way his hair curls
the same way yours does
away from the face
naturally
almost yourself
in an old photo
something maybe
about the hands
the way the elbows
on the knees
the way the cigarette
dangling
from those lips
and you are thinking
something's wrong with her explanation
something too familiar
in the eyes
the lowered eyelids
despite the smile
and you think
yes, there could be something
in all those lies—
something true
in black and white
luminous
and all-knowing
in those puffy, heavy-lidded eyes.

Sunlight On Oranges

in my grandmother's kitchen
each crystal of sugar
a prism of desire on my tongue
though she salted hers,
rivulets of juice
on her wrists, her fingers,
each plump segment
pried apart by the knife, the point
paring away flesh—
the navel—
she offered to me
saying it's what connected us
her mother
having died in childbirth
and mine, well
what little we know
maybe there were
some regrets
the social workers
never said much,
lies mostly
but now we have each other
and then her hands under mine at the piano
lifting my fingers
her voice in glassy arpeggios
like the wood thrush
and soon
the uncles on the porch,
the smell of tobacco and starch
in the cool, ironed sheets
and now the moon in the bed,
and me clinging
at first to the edge
of that hill
until sleep
lets me roll into her,
curl under that enormous arm,
and one day the tributaries,
the stain of raspberries
on my own hands

and on my own
granddaughter's mouth
brings it all back:
Love's first intoxication.

Rain

And my mother in the doorway
Next to me
Tsk-tsking
As the kids across the street
Splash naked
Through the morning
Their parents
Still asleep, oblivious
And the grass soaked
Windows streaked
The cinder street
A mirror of diamonds
Still unearthed
My heart, hiding there
Longs to leap,
Burst through this
Mesh of screen and bolts
That holds me
A fly
Caught
Between windows
Even at five
I understand
The crazed way
They dash themselves
Against the glass
I think I know that
Even when they
Are dead
Face down on the sill
Something will still
Glow
Green or blue
Like memory—
That gleam
In some distant
Time
That sets itself back
Into flight.

Thumbnails

I like the one of him
Stepping out of the airplane
Toward a fancy car on the runway

The one of his abs
Not so much
But then I prefer

A dad with a little more
Meat on his bones
But sure, he has a nice face

Striking, some would say;
And the one with the fake bullet hole
In his temple is really hilarious

A nice contrast
To the dude on the Harley—
Or to the one

With the little harem
Of babes
Ah, well, I find it all

Rather interesting
And the fact that
I look so much like him

The year he left my birth mom
For the secretary
And it took years for all of us to recover—

I'll not ask her
Which photo she prefers
Though the eyes

And certainly the jawline,
The arrogance in the mirror
Are unmistakably hers.

LockDown

When you don't know who you are
you can swim into
someone else's dreams
lounge on the pink chaise
by the piano
assuming there is a piano
an old upright
and you can tell the wife
her husband loves only you
he proved it that time
he engraved his initials and yours
on one of those locks
he padlocked to the grill work
on Pont Neuf
and threw the key into the Seine
but never mind, the Mayor
has issued an edict
the workers are seining
for all those keys
all seven hundred thousand million of them
the bridge having collapsed
under the weight of all that
love
all those hearts
in lock down
all that shiny brass
padlocked into one
giant metaphor
and you,
still locked here
in the illusion
that one day you will find
at least one strand of DNA
a small key
that will vault you
back
to some semblance of truth.

Promiscuity

When you don't know who you are
You figure you can fuck just about anybody
And it won't much matter
Seeing as how you've been fucked over your whole life already
But then your small town boyfriend
Pleads with you to please raise your shirt and you know right then
That despite his sweet face
You can't
You cannot, will not
Let some other kid be born
Who won't know who his/her
Parents are/aren't
And if you never do anything else
You will get yourself out of this hick town
And never look/come back
You will find any excuse possible
To forget who you aren't
And can never be
No matter who says you are
Until you at least figure out
Who the hell got you into this mess in the first damn place
So you can figure out how the hell
To get yourself back out.

The First Time

You meet your mom
The first thing
She asks are any of your kids dark?
And you say as in African-American? As in Hispanic?
As in gypsy or something?
And she in her Betty White hair
And Golden Girls getup
Says no, Indian
And you say as in India Indian?
And she says no, Navajo
And you flash back to that photo
Of yourself in fourth grade
Dressed up as Princess Summer Fall Winter Spring telling everyone
Who will listen that when you grow up you will be an Indian
You will live on the reservation
With Tonto and Silver
And furthermore
You have already practiced
Playing your Tom-Tom
In front of the mirror
While your other mom
Braids your hair
And exasperated, you
Wish to god grown ups
Would stop saying aww how damn cute
With her dark hair and dark eyes
Who knows?
She could be misinterpreted
And you stamp your foot
Because no one gets
That being talked about in the third person doesn't mean
That you don't really mean it
And why in hell
Can't they just understand
That you're not doing this
To be cute?
That you've already
Written to Broken Arrow and Chingachgook
And Cochise and Uncas
And as soon as they write back
You will have
All the proof that you or any of them need.

Epilogue

Not Your Daddy, he said
Not your old man
Not your papa
Not your Uncle
Get one thing straight
Your ma was a sucker
For a man in uniform
Not your fault
Don't get me wrong
There've been worse
But there've been better
And time
You stopped
Acting like
She gave two hoots
About you
Or that she would
If you came calling
Not that your old man
Would've lasted long
Even if he hadn't
Come home drunk
Once too often—
What wife wouldn't
Beat him over the head
With her high heel
Shoe—stiletto
Leave him for dead
The scent of some other woman?
You asked
So I decided might as well tell you
No sympathy from me
If he wasn't right in the head
After that
Handsome no-good
Now that you know
You really think
Your mother
Should've made any different
Decision?

Edge of the Earth

When the trucker
Opens his door for you
And motions
To the back seat
The road to the horizon
Is an oil slick
Doused with gasoline
Rainbows
And you figure
What the hell, anyway
Wriggling
Out of your skirt
And lifting your shirt
Up over your head
Like all the other
Truckers
Prefer
And if only that preacher
Could see you now
The one
Who sat by your bed
Lecturing you
On the merits
Of celibacy
His hand on his crotch
His eyes jackknifing
Like an eighteen wheeler
Over the map
Of your body
As if he was your Father
About to
Teach you
An unforgettable lesson.

Something in You Remembers

You are in Zanesville and the woman who runs the museum tells you that she will open it on Friday but only for children and when you tell her you have been coming here every year since you were a child she insists you are lying or she would remember. So you wait for her by the water wheel and when the river rises as high as the windows you float in over the transom but by then the woman is out in her garden trying to save the vegetables but the water in the museum is soaking the calendar and when you try to see if it is Friday the pages come off in your hands. Later, when you go back there the weight of it pulls you under.

You are in Cincinnati and the floors are black linoleum and the housekeeper has a fire in the stove but you don't understand until you try to pull your hand away and the skin comes off on the grating and you are screaming the whole time your father carries you home and the priest comes every day to try to make you stop crying and someone who says he is your grandfather puts his hand over your mouth so that he can get you to listen your grandfather is a judge and there are people in the other room who want to get married so he puts his glove over your hand so that you can't see it so you will be quiet. Later, when he and the priest come back, the people are already married and when he takes the glove off, your hand is still in it and they tell you this is what happens to naughty children.

You are in Westerville filling out the application when the woman who sells newspapers tells you she has seen your picture she knows you are the person who has been seeing her husband but when you tell her you have never been here she opens her purse and takes out the clipping and she tells you that people have warned her she can tell it is you by the way you hold the flowers. And when you get to the second page of the application someone has already filled out the section that says you do not fit in here so you put down the pen but the chain that is attached to the end of it breaks off in your hand and when you try to put it back

32

the man behind the counter won't let go of it. Later, when you are getting into the bus you find the newspapers have been set on fire but the words are made out of water.

No One Actually Said

She went to stay with an aunt
But that was the implication
Though they really
Sent her to the nuns
Who ran the asylum where
They kept the babies
That were only heads
Or were missing
Parts of bodies,
Brains
And the other 15-year-old
Unwed mothers
Screamed in labor
All the doors
Locked at night
So no one could escape
And the girls
Could figure out on their own
That this was a just punishment
For their sins
Especially, you know,
Adultery and lust
And if they really learned their lesson
They would
Relinquish their babies
To someone
Who really wanted them
Someone moral
And upstanding
With a clean house and apron
Who could see
To the upbringing
And if not, then, well
There were plenty
Of foster homes
Or orphanages
Where children
Learned to be useful
And obedient
Some even unto death,

And that being the case
Well, then the mother would
Just have to make the best of it.

Nobody, Too

How I envy the ease
with which my mother
vanished from my life
not unlike the way water
closes over a stone—
the same way light
disappears into shadow
in Monet's Argentieul
and men from the lives of women
in Wide Sargasso Sea.

I was five the year the school nurse
closed her fingers around my wrist,
a twig without the requisite rings
to identify the tree—

and the year I turned fifty
Damocles raised his sword
one last time
saying too bad
the law
was the law
and would not be unsealed

but by then I had already
mastered life's essential declensions:
I am;
I am not.

She Tried Everything, Really

To make me love her—
Expensive piano lessons,
A Bride Doll bigger
Than anyone else's,
The matching Mother-Daughter
Dresses.
And later the extravagant gifts
To my own children.
Make no mistake, though.
The forbidden topic
Was always there like a serpent
And we recoiled for different reasons.
One pull and I was Eve, Jezebel,
And Rahab rolled into one.
Devil's Daughter
Even the preacher mentioned Darkness
As if God himself
Meant blessed ignorance
Not innocence.
Lord knows
The Crusades themselves
Marched through our kitchen
Late one afternoon when I
Hurled the steak knives into the knife drawer faster than I
could dry them
While she washed
And refused to look at me
As if we were both to be called up
For the grand inquisition
Each of us certain
It was the other who deserved
The flames of Torquemada
But only one of us would be martyred.
The other a silent witness
To the horror.

Orange Shoes I Inherit from My Mother

Neither as brilliant or as supple
As the last Pope's red ones
Though the minute I see them
I KNOW I can forestall the convent
The idea of the Pope
Dancing!
These shoes
Tooled and cut
For fancy footwork
Like lace on fine linen—
Lord, when did my mother dance?
These are not nun's shoes!
Not quite Mary Janes nor huaraches
But just this side of flamenco
Tango—maybe or even tap
As if a Pope could or would
But maybe that's the best part
All the rumors, Speculation!
When he puts them on
He is Arthur Murray
Reincarnate
St. Fred Astaire right
Here on the steps of St Peter's
On this sweltering Sunday
Where we zumba for the multitudes
Just the two of us
His hand in mine
Instead of on the forehead
All the saints and martyrs
Shimmying
So Gloriously Inconceivable
Halleluiahs
Holy Father
In that flame eternal.

I Am Burning Some Things

ink crawling
from ancient bills, check stubs
crackling
iridescent insects
oozing
from the flames
fire ants fleeing her letters
scarabs more or less—
blue like a charm
an aunt once gave me
(someone said valuable)
all these papers
gold rimmed, weightless
heart and heat of dead
and living
watermark
rising up now
floating past
in winged vapors
incense
the soul
incised in Sanskrit

Armistice

Not a surrender—
Some of us eager
To leave
Others inclined
To tough it out
But life
Like a grenade
With the pin missing
And none of us
Willing
To get near enough
To examine
What we want to.

Improvisation on My Unknown Family

Lord knows
I want the heat of you
the wing, heartbeat, lub-dub
the blue hawk and soar
the dip backward
and trapeze swirl
the tricky jitter of bird-balance
between two reeds
and the hard bass line
the hot steel
rolling out of the foundry
a brain-vibrating blue
major minor diminished augmented
white keys
against your black
and more of
piano wire
unstrung / rewound
tacks on the felts
and barroom sound board
vibrato and the riff of you—
heads back
eyes closed
the down home willows weeping
and all those maple leaves
upside down
and drifting
in my direction.

Refraction

Like the moon
on late night
water

my memory of you
keeps breaking—

first light, then shadow
but always

the unbearable space

that holds the two
together

If Simon Were My Brother

I never asked
Though total strangers
Brought it up—
A definite resemblance
Nose, eyes, hair
Especially in that photo
Of me sandwiched
Between him and Itzhak
All of us faces gleaming
From a hot night of dance
And lightning streaks of color
Across our shirts
From an unsteady camera.
No idea where the photo went
Though I came across it
In our last move
Me changed so much
That I barely
Recognized myself
At first
Now that I look so much like
Someone else
I've never met,
Have yet to meet.

I never asked
Though total strangers
Brought it up—
A definite resemblance
Nose, eyes, hair
Especially in that photo
Of me sandwiched
Between him and Itzhak
All of our faces gleaming
From a hot night of dance
And lightning streaks of color
Across our shirts
From an unsteady camera.
No idea where the photo went
Though I came across it

43

In our last move
Me changed so much
That I barely
Recognized myself
At first
Now that I look so much like
Someone else
I've never met,
Have yet to meet.

Family Reunion, Not

And will someone stop them, please?
These little whiners   whirling in the garden
Who think they're the only
Theme and variation
Of the ancestors
As if they could ever dance   the way the old aunties did
Without
Their feet showing beneath their skirts
Or the uncles
Stripped to the waist   spurs flashing   leaping
So ridiculously high
One feared
They'd catch their boots   in their suspenders

Just who
Do they think they are?
These second cousins   of second cousins   twice removed
Who
Liar liar pants on fire
Say they know all about
How the old mothers   embroidered redbirds   tulip petals
And, God knows,
Mirrors!
Onto their petticoats
In stiches so cruel   their fingers bled
With the art as exacting
As a cardinal on the branch
Spreading its tail like a paper fan—
Enough already!

And how many times ho hum must we see Uncle Robert's face
In the third, fourth, sixth generation
Don't we know
They've heard all this already
A godzillion times
As if any of it ever mattered
I mean so what if he became a monk? Or a gravedigger?
Excuse me, butcher.

And so what do you say if we please, please, please

45

Please just this once
Skip the deep, dark discussion about all that DNA and Who
has what strain, what mole, what freckle
And for God's sake
Just get up and fucking start dancing?

As the Light Changes

you may be able to find
what you've been down on
your hands and knees all afternoon
searching for—
that blink that fell
from your eye when you
glanced out the window
just as you
opened the refrigerator
to take out the celery,
dipped the knife
into the peanut butter,
ran water into
your coffee cup.
oh, God, you are thinking
please don't
let my eyesight
go down the drain
like my mother's
please, please, please
don't remove
the center of the rose
so all that's left
are outer edges—
anything but that,
her bones old lace
her eyes filmed over
don't You dare
diss me
just because she
was an easy target,
a godamned martyr
always thinking she had to suffer,
well, I'm not
buying it
I'm down here
feeling every inch of this floor
for that piece of blue
that sits on the center
of my eyeball

and even if I have to
I will put glass in my own eye
before I let You
screw up my vision!

Rain, Doorway, Grief

So what is loss anyway
but the swagger of boys
in white suits
who brag about how heavy
the casket of their friend was
that stupid boy
who ran onto the highway
without looking both ways
as if he didn't know
that kids could die?

and so what if I don't like
the way they deface
the sky of my coloring book
with great slashes
of red like blood
saying clouds are nothing
but reflections anyway
so I might as well get over it?

and I might as well
get used to the fact
that it is my mother
who slammed our back door
against the dead boy's mom
who keeps coming back—
don't I know the other moms still
let her in their front doors even now
a year later
because they know
that mothers like mine
who have to adopt their kids
will never know
what it means
to lose something
they could never
forgive themselves for losing?

and so what if the gray
of my mother's eyes

49

clouds those things
we both should just always have known
in the first place?

[Chicago Poetry Center Juried Prize, 2010]

The Boy Who Once Walked Me Part Way Home

May have carried my books
Though I'd be surprised
If I let him
After the long pale schoolday
The weight of the chemistry text
In my own arms
To protect me
In case my mother
Tried to frighten him off with her
Wild imagination.
If I asked him about trajectories
He may have chosen basketball
To explain things
Or we may have discussed
Why he gave up the trombone
For football—
But mostly I worried
He'd had a fight with that other girl
The thin lanky one whose walk
I'd tried to imitate
Who was much better at small talk
And dark corner kisses
Whom I suspected he'd rather be with
As we crossed the intersection
And he turned in the direction
Of his house
And I to mine.

So Maybe We Should Have

just gone ahead
and fucked our brains out
and gotten it
over with,
out of our systems
demythologized
the whole romantic notion
that love has anything
to do with anything
but then I suppose
even if we had
you'd still want to know
if you were my brother
if I was calling things off
and I'd want you to be as miserable
as I
although we'd never really
gotten past a mild flirtation
a quiver of light
along the spines of the beach grass
one summer afternoon
as we sat looking out
at the water
the waves tumbling
over themselves like lion cubs
before the play
gets too rough
and the clouds
puffing along rather self-righteously
while you
pontificated about Bukowski
and the Beats
who I could never stand much
anyway but theories or no
you could make me laugh
even when others
used the word blowhard
in the same breath
whenever your name came up
but like antediluvian maps

with the four winds, no eight,
in the corners
and the sea monsters
laughing
I found you a rather charming
cartographer
charting your own territory
but then i remembered
the military maps
lining the walls of the Vatican
astonishingly accurate
considering the
ancient Romans
and good Catholic
that you were
eventually you
let the two-headed demon,
make you retreat even before
the sun
had a chance
to lower itself
into the water
yield itself to the night
which, I suppose,
would have been
a good time to start,
fucking, that is,
though I realize
just now that the word *sacred*
is just an anagram
of the word *scared*.

The Thing Is I Didn't Know

Which rooms had the mansions
Instead, my father's house
Seemed an embarrassment
Of smallness, a neglect of something greater
But one could, nevertheless
Stretch out on a well-worn sofa
With one's head hanging over the edge
To glimpse a lake of sky
Through mirrored window
Where blue seemed just this side of Prussian
And trees
Their birds holding themselves
Legendary in stillness.

Suddenly, Suddenly, You Here, the Blue Thread of You

As if seeing were believing
The blue stained glass of your eyes
Or the green of them, depending
On the slant of light
The cathedral of your heart
Again open with laughter
The noose of years forward and back
Swinging present, loosened
From absent, the doors repaired
The stain on the floor lifted
By some miracle
The windows swung wide—
The blind sighted,
The deaf hearing
The lame dancing.
Sometimes I see you on the street
The back of your head
The long, striding gait
A game, I think you have invented
Will not try to catch up to you
Must hoard these seconds
Believe you are still here
Refuse to visualize the sweater
Caught in the table saw
Not that!
The sleeve unraveling
Please, God, *no*!
I cannot go there, will not
You are yourself
Again
Among us
Not alone on the floor
Your heartbeats leaving you
One by one;
Only Dante knows
Which circle of hell
Not to write about
Could not fabricate
God/gods/goddesses
To lead us out

Replace the black holes
With stars
Align the planets
Roll back
The tsunami
Instead, you always receding
Taking us
With you—
If only, if only
Anything other than
These hearts
In ruins
Such beautiful ruins
The crazy iris of longing
Always
Pushing up
Through the rubble.

Early Morning

But the wind still sullen
After a sleepless night
I see it has toppled the lilac
Tangled the curtains
And just now the old love letters
skitter from the open desk
To the carpet
As if tempting me
To gather them in a heap
Just throw them out
And not worry if any are lost—
Like you
Like me.

Psalm

Even the stars in all their fury
Cannot deny
The calligraphy of trees
Scraping the night sky
Or the moon,
Trailing its hand
Through the water
Of your eyes
That distant fire—
Even the clouds
With their myriad gifts
Of purple and black
Open us to the heavens
At once lifting us up
Then setting us back down
Among our people—
That parallel universe
Where we don't quite
Ever
Really belong.

As the Crow Flies

On Fridays my grandmother
brought eggs still warm from the hen
and gossip from yesterday still "hot"
while Paul Harvey inside the radio
on the window ledge
blathered on about something—
Mattresses or whatever;
And my mother, happy to put down her mop
just listened.
and in the evening the mechanic from next door
came to sit on the porchstep
careful not to come all the way up
although he was invited
while the other neighbors
wandered over, too, after the supper dishes were cleared.

And sometimes in the middle of the afternoon
the preacher had been there,
rolled up his sleeves
and tied on an apron
and helped make the jam
or fold laundry because although
he was good at preaching
was uncomfortable with small talk—
and if you were lucky
he held your hand between his
as if it were a prayer
and so you were in love with him
because he looked like Martin Luther.

But at some point
the incessant gossip
was simply stale bread;
so, the surprise of moving to the Big City
was that the folks next door
came down off the porch,
put a blanket on the lawn
and said come on over—
and somewhere someone
on the next block

was playing Aretha whose voice
blasted over the back fence;
and the sound of the kanun
from the Toupouzians' window
hovered over the garden like a wish
while we all
crowded onto the blanket
drinking *Boone's Farm*
and swirling strawberries into cream
until the moon came up over the two-family flats
and hung in the elms like a gaslight
until midnight, that thief,
crept up
sent us home, our hearts
bursting with sorrow and gladness
and everyone's names
lingering
like strawberries on the tongue.

Genesis, Blue: An Ode to the Ancestors

Morning in mischief
And sun in a flash dance—
On spurs of light
My love comes to me
Flame coming to flame
To flare
In heat of sunrise.

And arise, thrush
In glassy arpeggio
Pizzicato of jay
Arise, jittering red-gold
Stars of morning
Dancing on branches
Arise, cardinals and Solomon birds
Scarlet honeycreepers
And crimson rosella
And you, red-winged blackbird
Preening in sunsplit water

And arise, skylarks swirling
Ascending and descending
In morning love poem
The wind in ecstasy
Teasing the tamaracks;

As swift as the waxwing,
My love gives chase among cedars
The reeds tremble
And leaves gasp
With his presence;

And arise, scarlet tanager
Arise, bunting
Painting this morning sky
With blue streaks
And red-green

Arise, honey bees
Wild with waiting,

61

Arise, sparrow in song dart

And arise, busy tailorbirds
Twittering in the branches
Sewing the leaves
For a sun cradle

And arise, hummingbird
Little stunt man
In green moccasins
Your breast
A blaze of topaz and fire opal

O, arise, horizonless morning
Your sun over the blue batik
Of new day,
Unfurling your
Blue silk
Over our shoulders.

Epilogue

When you don't know who you are
You can swim into someone else's dream
Or a million others'
Stroll across Pont Neuf
With the young, old
Hopeful, cynical
The lame
And bereft
All of us—Smitten
Temporarily insane
As if this were Lourdes
Lining up twelve deep
As if for a love mortgage
Fifteen-year ARM.
Or, God knows, thirty
If we get lucky
Bolting our Master Locks
Safety locks
Combination locks
Deadbolts
Affixed in pairs
Padlocking our future
All 4500 tons of it
To this fence
This bridge
Gay Paree
And tossing the key
Into the Seine
In solemn oath of foreverness
As if no one
Sees the multitude
Of divers
And nets
Seining
The bottom
Bringing up keys
Selling them
To the blind locksmith
Who, come night
Unlocks the fetters

The rune secrets
And unlatches Bill and Barbara
Chloe and Camille
Mum and Da
You and Me
To resell them
On the next bridge over
This one about to
Collapse under the weight of
All that
Love
All those hearts
In lockdown—
All that brass
Gleaming,
And the grillwork
Heavy with promise
All of it
About to be
Temporarily
Shut down.

JOHN B. BURROUGHS
EDITOR / PUBLISHER
JC@CRISISCHRONICLES.COM

3344 W 105TH STREET #4
CLEVELAND, OHIO 44111

(440) 315-0426

CRISIS CHRONICLES PRESS
VITAL INDEPENDENT LITERATURE SINCE 2008
HTTP://PRESS.CRISISCHRONICLES.COM

www.ingramcontent.com/pod-product-compliance
Lightning Source LLC
Chambersburg PA
CBHW071241090426
42736CB00014B/3177